Arctic Animals: Life Outside the Igloo

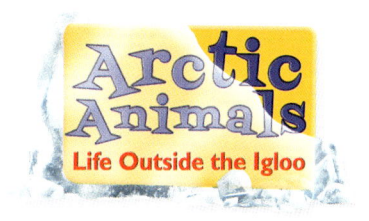

Snowshoe Hare

by Dee Phillips

Consultants:

Dr. L. Scott Mills
Professor, Department of Forestry and Environmental Resources, Program in Fisheries Wildlife and Conservation Biology, North Carolina State University, Raleigh, North Carolina

Kimberly Brenneman, PhD
National Institute for Early Education Research, Rutgers University, New Brunswick, New Jersey

BEARPORT PUBLISHING

New York, New York

Credits
Cover, © Donald M. Jones/Minden Pictures/FLPA; 2–3, © Howard Sandler/Shutterstock; 4T, © MVPhoto/Shutterstock; 4B, © studio23/Shutterstock; 5, © Donald M. Jones/Minden Pictures/FLPA; 7, © Michael Quinton/Minden Pictures/FLPA; 7R, © Dmitry Naumov/Shutterstock; 8T, © Tim UR/Shutterstock; 8B, © Sergei Drozd/Shutterstock; 9L, © Michael Quinton/Minden Pictures/FLPA; 9R, © Michael Quinton/Minden Pictures/FLPA; 10, © Jim Kravitz; 11, © Tom & Pat Leeson/Ardea; 12, © Hal Brindley/Shutterstock, © Paul Reeves Photography/Shutterstock, © FloridaStock/Shutterstock, and © Holly Kuchera/Shutterstock; 13, © MVPhoto/Shutterstock; 14, © Sumio Harada/Minden Pictures/FLPA; 15, © Martin Smart/Alamy; 16, © Alaska Stock/Alamy; 17, © Yva Momatiuk & John Eastcott/Minden Pictures/FLPA; 18, © Michael Quinton/Minden Pictures/FLPA; 19, © John Warden/Getty Images; 20T, © Cathy Hart/Alaska Stock/Alamy; 20B, © Tom Reichner/Shutterstock; 21, © MVPhoto/Shutterstock; 22TL, © Michael Quinton/Minden Pictures/FLPA; 22TR, © Andrew Millar/Alamy; 22BL, © Harri Taavetti/FLPA; 22BR, © Michelle Valberg/All Canada Photos/Alamy; 23TL, © Incredible Arctic/Shutterstock; 23TC, © MVPhoto/Shutterstock; 23TR, © Dmitry Naumov/Shutterstock; 23BL, © BGSmith/Shutterstock; 23BC, © Paul Reeves Photography/Shutterstock; 23BR, © Tom Reichner/Shutterstock; 24, © Michael Quinton/Minden Pictures/FLPA, © Andrew Millar/Alamy, © Harri Taavetti/FLPA, and © Michelle Valberg/All Canada Photos/Alamy.

Publisher: Kenn Goin
Creative Director: Spencer Brinker
Senior Editor: Joyce Tavolacci
Photo Researcher: Ruby Tuesday Ltd.

Library of Congress Cataloging-in-Publication Data

Phillips, Dee, 1967– author.
 Snowshoe hare / by Dee Phillips.
    pages cm. — (Arctic animals)
 Includes bibliographical references and index.
 ISBN 978-1-62724-527-2 (library binding) — ISBN 1-62724-527-8 (library binding)
 1. Snowshoe rabbit—Juvenile literature. 2. Hares—Juvenile literature. I. Title.
 QL737.L32P495 2015
 599.32'8—dc23
                2014035744

Copyright © 2015 Bearport Publishing Company, Inc. All rights reserved. No part of this publication may be reproduced in whole or in part, stored in any retrieval system, or transmitted in any form or by any means, electronic, mechanical, photocopying, recording, or otherwise, without written permission from the publisher.

For more information, write to Bearport Publishing Company, Inc., 45 West 21st Street, Suite 3B, New York, New York 10010. Printed in the United States of America.

10 9 8 7 6 5 4 3 2 1

Contents

Meet a Snowshoe Hare 4
Where Is Home? 6
Favorite Foods 8
Life in a Forest 10
Escaping from Enemies 12
White Fur 14
A New Coat 16
Baby Snowshoes 18
Growing Up 20

Science Lab 22
Science Words 23
Index 24
Read More 24
Learn More Online 24
About the Author 24

Meet a Snowshoe Hare

It's evening in a cold forest.

A fluffy white snowshoe hare is munching on twigs.

It hops from plant to plant over the snowy ground.

The hare doesn't sink into the soft, deep snow, though.

That's because its huge back feet work like snowshoes.

back foot

Snowshoe hares were named for their very large back feet, which help them walk on snow. The toes on a hare's back feet spread out to make the feet even bigger.

snowshoes

5

Where Is Home?

Snowshoe hares live in forests in Canada and the United States.

Some of these forests are in the **Arctic**.

The Arctic is farther north than any other area on Earth.

It's one of the coldest places in the world.

In winter, the weather in the Arctic can be colder than the inside of a freezer.

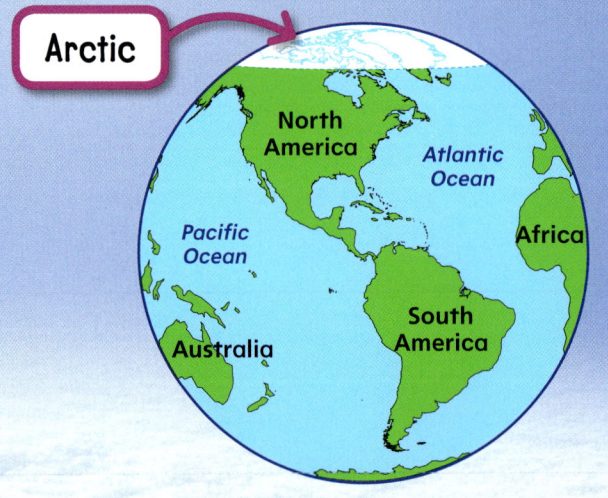

Where snowshoe hares live

Arctic

evergreen forest

a snowshoe hare covered with snow

Some snowshoe hares live in **evergreen** forests. Others live in forests where the trees lose their leaves in fall.

What kinds of food do you think snowshoe hares eat in a forest?

7

Favorite Foods

Snowshoe hares search for plants to eat in their forest homes.

In summer, the hares eat grasses and leaves from small bushes.

They also eat strawberry plants and wildflowers, such as bluebells.

In winter, snowshoe hares eat twigs.

Sometimes they chew and eat bark from tree trunks.

strawberry plant

bluebells

Snowshoe hares often stand up on their back legs to reach twigs and leaves that are high off the ground.

a snowshoe hare eating twigs

9

Life in a Forest

During the day, a snowshoe hare rests under a bush or log.

When evening comes, it leaves its resting place.

The hare spends the night hopping around the forest searching for food.

Then, in the morning, it finds another resting spot.

a snowshoe hare trail

A snowshoe hare uses the same trails to move around the forest every night. The hare uses these paths so much that the snow and ground get flattened.

a snowshoe hare resting under a bush

Escaping from Enemies

Every day, snowshoe hares face danger.

Predators, such as coyotes, lynxes, and foxes, hunt and eat hares.

Large birds, such as hawks and owls, swoop down and attack them.

If a hare sees a predator, it quickly hops away along one of its trails.

As it escapes, it can leap 9 feet (2.7 m) in a single hop!

Snowshoe Hare Predators

coyote

hawk

lynx

fox

As it hops, a snowshoe hare's big back feet move in front of its smaller front feet. The hare's back footprints always come before its front footprints.

Snowshoe hares hop away from enemies. They also have another way to stay safe. What do you think this could be?

13

White Fur

A snowshoe hare's white fur helps keep it safe from predators in winter.

Its white coat is good **camouflage**, helping it blend in with the snow.

If a predator gets close, the hare stays perfectly still.

Most of the time, enemies pass by without seeing the hare.

a snowshoe hare blending in with the snow

What do you think happens to a snowshoe hare's coat in spring after the snow melts?

A hare's white coat isn't just good camouflage. The coat is also very thick. It keeps the hare warm and protects it from the freezing cold temperatures.

15

A New Coat

When spring arrives, a snowshoe hare's white coat starts to **shed,** or fall out.

At the same time, the animal grows a new, brownish-gray coat.

Just like its winter coat, this new coat helps the hare hide from predators.

Now it can blend in with logs and dry leaves on the forest floor.

This hare's white fur is shedding, and its summer coat is growing in.

An adult snowshoe hare is about the size of a cat. It weighs up to 4 pounds (1.8 kg).

brownish-gray summer coat

17

Baby Snowshoes

Spring is also the time when male and female hares meet up to **mate**.

About five weeks after mating, a female gives birth to up to six babies.

The tiny hares are born on the ground among the forest plants.

Just a few hours after they are born, the babies are able to hop.

Each baby hare finds a safe, cozy place in which to hide from predators.

a baby snowshoe hare peeking from its hiding place in a hollow log

a three-week-old snowshoe hare

A mother hare feeds her babies with milk from her body. The babies are called leverets.

A newborn snowshoe hare weighs about 2 ounces (57 g). Hold a tennis ball in your hand. The ball weighs about the same as a baby hare.

19

Growing Up

Just a few days after they are born, the babies start to eat plants.

At four weeks old, they can take care of themselves and they leave their mother.

When fall arrives, each young hare grows a thick white coat.

Now it's ready for its first winter as a grown-up snowshoe hare!

a young snowshoe hare eating plants

a young hare growing its first white winter coat

A female snowshoe hare starts to have babies when she is one year old. She may give birth to up to four litters of babies each summer.

a fully grown snowshoe hare

21

Science Lab

Animal Hide-and-Seek

A snowshoe hare's fur acts as camouflage. It helps the hare hide from predators. Some animals use camouflage in another way. They use it to help them sneak up on the animals they hunt!

Try to spot the hidden animal in each of the four pictures. See if you can find an owl, a bobcat, a snowshoe hare, and a bird called a rock ptarmigan.

1.
2.
3.
4.

Which of the animals do you think use camouflage to hide from predators?

Which use their camouflage to stay hidden while hunting for prey?

(The answers are on page 24.)

22

Science Words

Arctic (ARK-tik) the northernmost area on Earth, which includes the Arctic Ocean and the North Pole

camouflage (KAM-uh-flahzh) the colors and markings on an animal that help it blend in with its surroundings

evergreen (EV-ur-green) plants that stay green throughout the year and don't lose their leaves

mate (MAYT) to come together in order to have young

predators (PRED-uh-turz) animals that hunt and eat other animals

shed (SHED) to have an old coat of fur fall out

23

Index

Arctic 6
baby hares 18–19, 20–21
camouflage 14–15, 16–17, 22
feet 4, 13
food 4, 7, 8–9, 10, 19, 20

forests 4, 6–7, 8, 10
fur 14–15, 16–17, 20, 22
hopping 4, 10, 12–13, 18
mating 18
milk 19

predators 12–13, 14, 16, 18, 22
resting 10–11
trails 10, 12
weather 6, 15
weight 17, 19

Read More

Frost, Helen. *Arctic Hares (Pebble: Polar Animals).* Mankato, MN: Capstone (2007).

Robbins, Lynette. *Rabbits and Hares (Jump!).* New York: PowerKids Press (2012).

Shea, Therese M. *Arctic Hares (Animals That Live in the Tundra).* New York: Gareth Stevens (2010).

Learn More Online

To learn more about snowshoe hares, visit www.bearportpublishing.com/ArcticAnimals

About the Author

Dee Phillips lives near the ocean on the southwest coast of England. She develops and writes nonfiction and fiction books for children of all ages.

Answers for page 22

1) A bobcat
2) A rock ptarmigan 
3) A great gray owl 
4) A snowshoe hare 

The hare and ptarmigan have camouflage to help them hide from predators. The bobcat and owl have camouflage to hide from the animals they hunt.